THE POTLUCK HALL OF FAME
& Other Bizarre Christian Lists

David Dickerson

Cartoons by Mary Chambers

INTERVARSITY PRESS
DOWNERS GROVE, ILLINOIS 60515

For Mom and Dad

Text: © 1992 by David Dickerson

Cartoons: © 1992 by Mary Chambers

InterVarsity Press is the book-publishing division of InterVarsity Christian Fellowship, a student movement active on campus at hundreds of universities, colleges and schools of nursing in the United States of America, and a member movement of the International Fellowship of Evangelical Students. For information about local and regional activities, write Public Relations Dept., InterVarsity Christian Fellowship, 6400 Schroeder Rd., P.O. Box 7895, Madison, WI 53707-7895.

Cover illustration: Mary Chambers

ISBN 0-8308-1832-4

Printed in the United States of America ∞

Library of Congress Cataloging-in-Publication Data
Dickerson, David.
    The potluck hall of fame/David Dickerson: with cartoons by Mary
Chambers.
        p.   cm.
   ISBN 0-8308-1832-4
   1. Christian life—Humor.   I. Title.
  BV4517.D53 1992
  202'.07—dc20   *92-12377*
                                                         CIP

15	14	13	12	11	10	9	8	7	6	5	4	3	2	1
04	03	02	01	00	99	98	97	96	95	94	93	92		

Top Ten Ways to Make Evangelicals Nervous Without Actually Sinning

10. Smoke a pipe (just like C. S. Lewis!).

9. Get a tattoo.

8. Burn incense.

7. Have an extensive rock music collection.

6. Wear a cross with Jesus still hanging from it.

5. Be an artist.

4. Keep beer in the refrigerator.

3. Subscribe to the *Christian Century*.

2. Wear a peace symbol.

1. Make jokes about evangelicals.

TOP THREE ENTRIES IN THE POTLUCK HALL OF FAME

*these are all verifiably true though the actual names of the honorees have been mercifully deleted

THE LADY WHO BROUGHT STEW IN A DIAPER PAIL

THE COUPLE WHO TRANSPORTED FOOD IN THE TRUNK OF THEIR CAR WITH THE LEAKY EXHAUST, GIVING EVERYTHING THE DISTINCT FLAVOR OF GASOLINE

THE LITTLE OLD LADY WHO MADE HER TUNA CASSEROLE WITH KAL-KAN®

Top Ten Christian Athlete's Excuses

10. The light of Truth got in my eyes.

9. The other team must have prayed harder.

8. The quarterback gave signals in tongues, and there was no interpretation.

7. I expected the referee to be judging on grace rather than works.

6. While I was running with patience the race set before me, all the unbelievers seemed eager to finish.

5. Our opponents were called the *Devils,* so we assumed they *had* to lose.

4. I've been missing my quiet times lately.

3. I got the play diagrams confused with a map of Paul's missionary journeys.

2. We are Christians, and we didn't want to offend them by winning.

1. Maybe our losing will help some of them come to Christ.

Top Ten Reasons Churches Don't Ask Clown Ministries to Return

10. They force people to smile during the 8 a.m. service.

9. It's hard to say with dignity, "The sermon today will be given by Brother Umpa-Doody."

8. Whoopee cushions inevitably appear under the pew cushions.

7. Sermons take a lot longer when they're in pantomime.

6. Clowns wearing blue curly wigs might be confused with elderly women.

5. Many denominations do not recognize seltzer-water baptism.

4. Dribble glasses might be used during the communion service.

3. They have to pay janitors extra to get silly string off the ceiling.

2. The junior-highers pop their balloons during closing prayer.

1. They realize they have enough clowns working there already.

TOP THREE
PRETTY GOOD REASONS
TO WORK IN THE NURSERY

YOU DIDN'T HAVE TIME
TO IRON YOUR CLOTHES

THE SERMON LOOKS
ESPECIALLY POOR

YOU HAD BEANS FOR SUPPER

Top Seven Questions Atheists Ask

7. If God is truly just, why does *The Door* stay in business?

6. How can I tell if I've crossed the line of despair?

5. Do I *have* to believe in predestination?

4. How many angels can dance on Bultmann's grave?

3. When we're resurrected, will our bodies really glow in the dark?

2. Is there some easy way I can arrive at truth without having to spend a whole lot of time thinking about it?

1. Who does God say will win the next Super Bowl?

Things Christians Can Do That Don't Involve Smoking, Drinking, Dancing, Swearing, Gambling or Sinning

2. Eat.

1. Have children.

Nine Worst Sins You Can Commit While Bowling

9. Envy—from seeing how other people seem to bowl without looking stupid.

8. Lust—from looking at overweight people in polyester slacks with those oh-so-sexy shoes.

7. Pride—from being able to get the ball almost to the pins before it goes into the gutter.

6. Gluttony—from not being able to get enough of those nachos dipped in lukewarm American cheese.

5. Sloth—because bowling balls are *heavy!*

4. Whatever the sin against the Holy Spirit is, you can probably do it in a bowling alley.

3. Murder—particularly if you're a lousy player and let go of the ball at a bad time.

2. Theft. (Although if you take someone else's bowling shoes, they'll probably thank you.)

1. Math anxiety. (It's not exactly a sin, but who needs it?)

Top Ten Fears Teens Have About Christian Camps

10. The food will move when I'm not looking.
 9. They'll make us play that stupid relay with the toothpicks and Lifesavers.
 8. We'll take a moonlight hike through some poison ivy.
 7. They'll serve beans right before the talent show.
 6. We'll have to wear dorky chips of wood with our names on them.
 5. The speaker will be a barely literate ex-football player who can't take a joke.
 4. There won't be a panty raid.
 3. They'll find out that Mom wrote my name on my underwear.
 2. The bonfire will rage out of control while everyone's head is bowed.
 1. I'll meet a girl/guy who lives in another state, fall in love, end the week with a big kiss, promise to write, write maybe three letters, and then meet them ten years later while on vacation and not know what to say.

THREE WORST PLAGUES UNLEASHED
UPON UNREPENTANT WILFORD, IOWA

POTHOLES

SWARMS OF LAWN ORNAMENTS

WINDCHIMES

Ten Products Most Commonly Found in the Old-Fashioned Values Store

10. Pictures of Jesus with eyes that follow you across the room.

9. Hide-bound Bibles (King James Version).

8. Norman Lear punching bags.

7. Genuine hand-carved spanking paddles.

6. Christian sex-education books with the offensive material edited.

5. "No Credit Cards Accepted" signs.

4. "Can Single Working Mothers Really Be Christian?" pamphlets.

3. Books entitled *Wives Who Are Assertive and the Men Who Let It Happen*.

2. The "100% Pure Thoughts All Day" Bible calendar.

1. Secular humanist dolls (made of straw).

Top Ten Christian Musical Flops

10. *Hello Paulie!* (A Musical Missionary Journey)

9. *South Samaria*

8. *The Sound of No Music* (An *a cappella* history of the Church of Christ)

7. *Jesus Christ, Disco Star*

6. *West Bank Story*

5. *The King, the Son, the Holy Spirit, and I*

4. *The Best Little Brothel in Gomorrah*

3. *Sunday in the Living Room with Pat*

2. *Noah!* (aka *Bye Bye Birdie)*

1. *Redeemed Yankees*

Top Eight Articles from Christian Women's Magazines

8. "Dressing for Pastoral Visitation—A New Fashion Report"

7. "Avoiding Marital Conflict through Violent Housework"

6. "Pregnancy: What It Is, and How You Can Get It"

5. "How Submissive Are You? Take This Fun Quiz! Now."

4. "Kitty-bear Got Hit By a Truck! A Drama in Real Life"

3. "100 Cute Household Crafts You Can Make from Old Church Bulletins"

2. "Home Schooling: Getting Your Husband to Do It"

1. "Three Charming Patterns for Christian Toilet Seat Covers"

Top Seven Seminary Party Jokes

7. Knock-knock.

Who's there?

Saint Jude.

Saint Jude who?

Saint Jude rather ask questions than let an apostle into your house, you must have gone to Harvard Divinity School.

6. Q: What do you get when you cross a Jehovah's Witness with a Unitarian?

A: A knock at the door for no apparent reason.

5. A man came to a famous preacher for counseling. He said, "I'm in a terrible bind, pastor. I'm caught between the devil and the deep blue sea!"

"Are you a Christian?" the preacher asked.

"No," the man admitted.

"Then you'd better risk the deep blue sea."

4. Two premillennialists walk into an amillennial bar, and the bartender looks up and says, "Are you guys still here?"

3. Q: How many Presbyterians does it take to change a light bulb?

A: There are fifteen people on the Light Bulb Replacement Sub-Committee, three people are in charge of refreshments, and the meetings are conducted decently and in order, but the light bulb never actually gets changed.

2. A seminarian invited a friend to come see his new parrot. During the visit, the bird kept saying, "Who? Who?"

"My gosh," the guest commented. "What with its wide, puzzled eyes and the sound it was making, I thought it was an owl."

"No, it's a parrot all right," the host said. "I just read to him from Kierkegaard."

1. Q: What do you get when you cross an insomniac, a dyslexic and an agnostic?

A: "Someone who lies awake at night wondering if there is a dog."

TOP THREE
PASTOR'S GREETING CARDS

Where have you been
the past 9 weeks?
(Don't tell me on vacation!)

If you're not here
Next Sunday
You'll be my
Sermon illustration

Our numbers had been dwindling
And visitors were few

Lightning struck our steeple
And the staff all had the flu

Plague had closed the nursery
What else was there to do?

SOMEONE AMONG US
MUST HAVE SINNED
We cast lots and it was you

Thank you for your prophecy
How nice of you to tell us
How God intends to
send us all to Hell
Where He can't smell us

Top Nine Sermon Tapes to Avoid

9. "What's Wrong with America Today—part 3 of 9"

8. (tie) "The End Is Still Near"

 "Who Is the Beast? Let Me Tell You"

7. "Why God Is Fed Up with All of You"

6. "If Jesus Were Alive Today, How Would He Vote?"

5. *"Kenosis* in Philippians: A Hermeneutical Approach to the Pauline *Weltanschauung"*

4. "Rock Music: The Horrible Things Your Children Shouldn't Be Listening to That I'm Going to Tell You About in Detail"

3. "Militarism in the Bible: A Feminist Critique"

2. "Fun with Numbers (and Deuteronomy Too!)"

1. "How I Spent My Paid Vacation to the Holy Land"

TOP THREE THINGS FOR KIDS TO DO AFTER CHURCH WHILE THEIR PARENTS VISIT

CHASE EACH OTHER AROUND THE PARKING LOT CAUSING DRIVERS TO SIN

SEE IF YOU CAN GET YOUR OFFERING BACK

INVITE A BUNCH OF PEOPLE HOME FOR LUNCH

Top Ten Excuses for Missing Bible Study

10. I didn't feel led to attend.

9. My horoscope said it was a bad idea.

8. I stayed up late last night not converting a friend.

7. My fellowship group was playing "Twister" that night.

6. I've already read the Bible.

5. I was busy praying about the church's apathy.

4. There was a "Flying Nun"-a-thon on cable.

3. I had a visitation from God and lost track of the time.

2. There was an altar call at my church and they played all the verses of "Just As I Am," so I was detained for three days.

1. Saint Paul and I don't always agree.

The Six Most Popular Subjects of Christian Art

6. Jesus smiling.

5. Jesus praying/depressed.

4. Jesus on the cross.

3. Jesus with children.

2. Christian rock group posters.

And one that's not art:

1. Teddy-bear magnets holding heart-shaped balloons containing thought-provoking messages, for example, "I can't BEAR to be without Jesus!!"

Top Ten Christian Pick-Up Lines

10. "I hear there's going to be a love offering tonight."

9. "Just looking at you makes me feel all ecumenical."

8. "Do you believe in predestination?"

7. "I'm pretty flexible. I don't think a woman should be submissive on the first date."

6. "I'm strongly into relationship evangelism."

5. "You have the looks of Amy Grant and the soul of Mother Teresa." *(Don't* mix these up!)

4. "I don't see it myself, but people tell me I resemble Michael W. Smith."

3. "What do you think Paul meant when he said, 'Greet everybody with a holy kiss'?"

2. "Did I tell you that my great-uncle was a *personal friend* of C. S. Lewis?"

1. "I just don't feel called to celibacy."

THREE POPULAR WAYS TO DECORATE WITH V.B.S. CRAFTS

YOU CAN NEVER HAVE ENOUGH AEROSOL LIDS FILLED WITH PLASTER AND A PLASTIC FORK TO HOLD ALL OF YOUR "RECIPE FOR A HAPPY HOME" CARDS

picture frames

paper plates

sun visors

old jars

your Bible →

ANYTHING WITH MACARONI GLUED ON IT IS A GUARANTEED HIT

A TRASH CAN MADE FROM STYROFOAM EGG CARTONS IS A GIFT THAT WILL LAST A LIFETIME

The Thirteen Most Obscure Biblical Names That Turn up in Crossword Puzzles

CLIP 'N' SAVE for Handy Reference!

13. DOEG
12. EBAL
11. ENON
10. HETH
9. IRAD
8. JADA
7. KISH
6. MASH
5. OREB
4. OZEM
3. ULAM
2. UNAM
1. URIA

Ten Most Common Subjects for Youth Speakers' Opening Jokes

(Warning: Do not read this list within a half-hour of eating a large meal.)

10. Passing gas
9. Boogers
8. Going to the bathroom
7. Someone laughing so hard that milk comes out of their nose
6. Throwing up
5. Diarrhea
4. Someone meeting St. Peter at the gate of heaven (usually making fun of the sinfulness of the nearest competing youth director)
3. Acne
2. Having your fly open
1. Passing gas

The Ten Least Popular Precious Children Figurines

10. "Lord, I Broke My Nose"

9. "Will Someone Shut That Baby Up?"

8. "The Li'l Inquisitor"

7. "Gosh Darn These Pimples"

6. (tie) "The Butterfly Collector"

         "It's Still Wiggling!"

5. "Where Do Babies Come From?"

4. "From My Heart to Yours: The Blood Transfusion"

3. "Thank God for Baby Scorpions"

2. "The Precious Pieta"

1. "Lord, I've Sentimentalized the Gospel for Money"

Top Ten Titles for Christian Golf Videos

10. *God Is My Caddy*

9. *The Five Iron in a Fallen World*

8. *Pray Your Way to the PGA*

7. *Golfing the Stations of the Cross*

6. *He Who Controls the Lightning*

5. *Mounting Up with Eagles*

4. *Putt Till We're Raptured!*

3. *Aim for the Steeple* (miniature golf only)

2. *Which Club Would Jesus Use?*

1. *Fill My Cup, Lord*

Top Ten Changes in the Church by 2050

10. Holographic manger scenes.

9. Short-term missions trips to Venus.

8. Reclining pews.

7. Bread *and* wine in one tiny pill!

6. Offering plates accept credit cards.

5. Microfilm Bibles can be lost in a million more places than presently possible.

4. Fewer babies crying in church due to viability of cloning.

3. Laser slide shows in sensurround.

2. Robot evangelists—many will be indistinguishable from the real thing!

1. Photocopiers that don't break down.

Top Ten Difficulties Faced by Christian Vampires

10. Can't wear cross without risking ugly burn scars.

9. At potlucks, someone always cooks with garlic.

8. Church work days are usually held when the sun is out.

7. Don't understand Pauline reference to "seeing in a glass, darkly."

6. Communion isn't *really* someone's blood.

5. Janitor gets suspicious when you hang around the belfry.

4. Have to take large bulky coffin along on missionary trips.

3. Preschool kids who run with stakes.

2. Fangs cause lisping during the "trespasses" part of The Lord's Prayer.

1. When you're immortal, it's hard to find one really good church and stick with it.

PASTOR'S NIGHTMARE #9

Top Ten Televangelists' Pet Peeves

10. Toupees that look fake no matter how much Brylcream you add.

9. Being made fun of by people who can't get a Southern accent right.

8. When God tells you you're going to become president and you find out later that he lied to you.

7. Faulty doghouse air conditioning.

6. "Miracle Healing Towels" that still have "Tulsa Hilton" written on them.

5. When at the stroke of midnight you've raised $7,999,999 for God, and he kills you anyway.

4. The passages of the Bible that have big words.

3. Declining sales of "Christ's Own Salad Dressing."

2. Mother is sometimes stubborn about keeping her pension check.

1. Prison food.

The Top Eleven Christian Bumper Stickers You're Never Going to See

11. DON'T FOLLOW ME. I'M PROBABLY GOING TO A POTLUCK.
10. CATHOLICS HAVE MORE MASS.
9. GOD SAID IT. I BELIEVE IT. SO YOU SHUT UP.
8. I FOUND IT, WHATEVER IT IS.
7. I HAVE GOD IN MY CAR, SO DRIVE CAREFULLY.
6. CHRISTIANS AREN'T PERFECT; THEY JUST ACT LIKE IT SOMETIMES.
5. I ♥ DISPENSATIONAL ESCHATOLOGY.
4. ALL THIS AND HEAVEN TOO.
3. PRE-TRIBBERS HAVE MORE FUN.
2. IN CASE OF RAPTURE, THIS CAR HAS CRUISE CONTROL.
1. PREDESTINATION HAPPENS.

Top Ten Signs of the Apocalypse

10. All the water in the world develops that diet-soda aftertaste.

9. Satan appears on Letterman to talk about his new movie entitled *The End of the World Is Coming Soon.*

8. Christ's face appears on a tortilla in Mexico City—and he's frowning!

7. The sun loses one-third of its light, the moon loses one-third of its light, and the PTL Club loses one-third of its Nielsen ratings.

6. Scientists discover that bran is bad for you too.

5. The Pope stops wearing that funny hat.

4. Pat Robertson runs for president on the Democratic ticket.

3. Credit-card companies start sending college graduates junk mail *every single day.*

2. Shops nationwide begin to close early so that their employees can make it home before the nightly swarms of giant man-eating locusts.

1. The world's number-one growth industry is tattooing.

TOP THREE SCRIPTURES MOTHERS LOVE TO QUOTE

CLEANLINESS IS NEXT TO GODLINESS

THE LORD HELPS THOSE WHO HELP THEMSELVES

STAY OUT OF THE WATER FOR 30 MIN. AFTER EATING

Top Ten Lines Christian Women Use to Break Up

10. I've found someone more spiritual.

9. It's not God's will.

8. I feel called to mission work very far away from you as soon as possible.

7. It could never work—I'm sanguine and you're phlegmatic.

6. God loves me and *must* have a better plan for my life.

5. I feel like I'm dating my brother.

4. At least I got a lot out of our Bible studies together.

3. You need someone with lower standards.

2. I think we should just be prayer partners.

1. I *do* love you, but it's just *agape* love now.

Ten Animals Not Taken on the Ark

10. The marsupial whose pancreas is a cure for cancer.

 9. Unicorns.

 8. Brontosauri.

 7. The rare bird that dies when it gets crowded.

 6. The purple-tufted ark eater.

 5. The Himalayan legless ostrich.

 4. The red polar bear.

 3. The paisley-patterned chia pet.

 2. The really tacky butterfly.

 1. Cockroaches (they survived anyway).

Top Nine Things Overheard at the Religious Broadcaster's Convention

9. (tie) "Is that your *real* hair?"

"You're much less funny-looking in person."

8. "God wanted *me* to die, too, but I just slipped him a million and kept my mouth shut."

7. "I hear 'The Pastor Bob Show' is going to add an animated clown named Tuggles."

6. "Oh, about 20 million, after taxes. Oh, I forgot. . . . I don't *pay* any taxes."

5. "Grits! . . . Get your red-hot grits here. . . ."

4. "I sold my soul to Satan and my ratings went up, but now I have bad dreams."

3. "I hear God's going back to his trimmed-beard look."

2. "I got some great pictures of you at the Radisson. . . . No, ten thousand will do for now."

1. "Look at that thin, hairy guy over there. He must be new."

Top Nine Ways to Tell If You're Possessed

9. You're irritable and tense and have horns growing out of your head.

8. Inconvenient levitation at family gatherings.

7. The voices in your head sing "Sympathy for the Devil" instead of "Feelings."

6. You find yourself crank calling the Crystal Cathedral and shouting, "No you can't! No you can't!" into the phone.

5. You sometimes feel drowsy in church.

4. You enjoy suffering so much you actually watch soap operas and Cubs games.

3. When you laugh really hard, acid comes out your nose.

2. During daily devotions you tend to burst into flames.

1. The red light goes on when you test yourself in a possess-o-meter.

Top Seven Religious Movies Coming Out of Hollywood Soon

7. *Vacation Bible School Massacre IV*

6. *Jesus: A Heck of a Guy*

5. *Leviticus* (A sequel to *Exodus,* but not as interesting)

4. *The Scarlet Letter*

3. *I Was a Teenage Baptist*

2. *John Donne: The Early Years*

1. *Bad Habits* (When these sisters get mad, the mob had better look out!)

Top Ten Christian Turn-Ons

10. Coed Bible studies.

9. Chinese food and walks in the rain.

8. Diaphanous choir robes.

7. Christopher Parkening's recording of *Jesu, Joy of Man's Desiring*.

6. The scene in *It's a Wonderful Life* when everyone jumps in the pool.

5. The 7th verse of "Just As I Am."

4. Song of Songs in the original Hebrew.

3. Stained-glass portraits of Joan of Arc.

2. Frankincense.

1. "One cup" communion services.

Top Nine Ways to Make Full Immersion Baptism More Interesting

9. Add fish and a little deep-sea-diver statue.

8. Add a wave machine.

7. Make it a dunk tank. The congregation throws softballs.

6. Give prize to whoever goes under the longest and lives.

5. Add floating squeaky toys.

4. Use a water slide!

3. Don't provide towels. To dry off, the baptisee has to hug people in the congregation.

2. Color the water orange.

1. Do it to infants.

TOP THREE EXAMPLES
OF RARE BAPTISTRY ART

WAIKIKI BEACH

LOUISIANA BAYOU

GLACIER BAY

Top Ten Duties of Christians Who Work for the CIA

10. Guard the White House mint dish.

9. Wiretap the nursery.

8. Walk the President's dog.

7. Make up cool Biblical codenames (Example: JERICHO).

6. Vacuum.

5. Leave tracts at embassy parties.

4. Sit around and avoid starting coups.

3. Trick foreign spies into attending Bible studies.

2. Taste the president's food (the non-Christians drink his alcohol).

1. Short-sheet foreign leaders' beds.

Top Four Verses Christians Wonder About

4. "Even the handle sank in after the blade, which came out his back. Ehud did not pull the sword out, and the fat closed in over it" (Judges 3:22).

3. "Do not answer a fool according to his folly, or you will be like him yourself. Answer a fool according to his folly, or he will be wise in his own eyes" (Proverbs 26:4-5).

2. "Your teeth are like a flock of sheep just shorn, coming up from the washing. . . . Your temples behind your veil are like the halves of a pomegranate. . . . All beautiful you are, my darling; there is no flaw in you" (Song of Songs 4:2-7),

1. "But even the archangel Michael, when he was arguing with the devil about the body of Moses . . . said, 'The LORD rebuke you!' " (Jude 9).

Top Nine Faith Healer Pet Peeves

9. Stagehands who forget when to pull the fishing line.

8. Contracting embarrassing rashes.

7. When the Actors Union strikes.

6. People who are too weak to take a little shove in the head.

5. Arteriosclerosis and other maladies that are hard to say on-camera.

4. Occasional embarrassing laying on of hands around the waistline.

3. When you're trying to preach, there are always sick people coughing.

2. Crybabies.

1. (tie) When it turns out *everybody* in the audience has one leg shorter than the other.
When these people object to having their legs pulled.

Ten Features of the New McChurch

10. Tithe comes with money-back guarantee.

9. Drive-thru services.

8. Sacramental wine served in refillable Gerbert mug.

7. Communion wafers are broiled, not fried.

6. Scratch off your program and get a prize!

5. Sermons come in 35-second sound bites.

4. Nondenominational wallpaper.

3. Ushers wear striped polyester shirts and green baseball caps.

2. After baptism warm-air hand driers are available.

1. Exit doors say, "Thank You."

Top Nine Comments Overheard on the Ark

9. "Has anyone seen the termites?"

8. "Japheth, it's your turn to clean out the pachyderm section."

7. "You fool! You fed the *Alligator* Chow to the *crocodiles*!"

6. "Wake up. The cats and dogs are at it again."

5. "How was I supposed to know the camels would shed?"

4. "Hmm . . . tastes like chicken."

3. "The mice can get seasick; it's the hippos I worry about."

2. "Yuk! Bugs!"

1. "After this, I'll be *glad* to go hunting."

TEN THINGS WE CAN KNOW ABOUT GOD
(JUST BY ASKING LUTER AND LILA DEAN SMELTY)

Well, for one, we know he hates facial hair

He wouldn't be caught dead in a Toyota

Men who use hair spray disgust Him

Can't say He'd approve of that new carpet

He likes to be out by noon on Sundays

He won't allow hand puppets in the sanctuary

He'd steer clear of all this low-fat, low-cholesterol new age food

His favorite color is blue

He thinks plastic houseplants are o.k.

He likes exactly the same kind of music as me & Luter

chambers

Job's Top Ten Pet Peeves

10. Friends who tell you to curse God and die, even after you've explained that that would be unbiblical.

9. Blisters that itch.

8. High cost of sackcloth and ashes.

7. People who cut ahead of you in the express lane with thirteen items.

6. Running out of pottery on a really boil-laden day.

5. Being God's chosen.

4. Doctors who say, "There's nothing wrong with you. Curse God and die."

3. Having to clean up all those dead cattle.

2. Mondays.

1. People who keep quoting Romans 8:28 at you.

Top Twelve Christian Vanity Plates

12. URA SNR
11. JON 316
10. PRETRIB
9. I TITHE
8. CLVNST
7. NEW JEW
6. PTL 700
5. FUNDY
4. GODS VW
3. IXOYE
2. PAT 1996
1. DIED 4U

The Nine Least Popular Hymns

9. "Please, God, Don't Hurt Me"

8. "Lenin Is the Antichrist"

7. "Softly and Tenderly, Cholesterol Builds Up in Your Arteries"

6. "The Purgatory Shuffle"

5. "Leviticus Chapter Seventeen"

4. "Footprints" (to the tune of "How Great Thou Art")

3. "It's Good for Us to Suffer, Suffer"

2. "Loot the Towns, and Sack the Cities" (The Crusaders' Hymn)

1. "Apostle Peter Popped a Pack of Papist Preachers"

Noah's Top Ten Pet Peeves

10. Surly carnivores in tight quarters.

9. Monkeys who evolve, and then don't give you any credit.

8. No retirement, even at 600 years.

7. Reports of your kid getting teased at school because he's a Jew named *Ham*.

6. Having only one window (no ventilation).

5. Not being able to remember whether it's "mongooses" or "mongeese."

4. Moulting season.

3. When your kids keep saying, "Are we there yet?"

2. Stores that don't sell gopherwood by the cubit.

1. When, on the thirtieth rainy day in a row, somebody suggests playing "Spoons" again.

Top Ten Christian Products Currently in Development

10. Brylcreem solvent.

9. Flag polish.

8. Life-size inflatable Tony Campolo doll.

7. Tupperware Bible cover.

6. Blush-hiding makeup (helpful for when you start to use canned sales pitches on your friends).

5. Prayer-cloth wringer.

4. Automatic see-no-evil sunglasses.

3. Patriotism-in-a-can.

2. After-the-Junior-High-School-All-Nighter-Clean-Up-Spray (exorcism tested!).

1. Electronic potluck-dish identifier.

THREE WAYS TO TELL IF YOUR CHILD
IS DESTINED FOR THE MINISTRY

YOUR FIRST CLUES CAN
COME VERY EARLY

MAY HAVE TROUBLE
SLEEPING ON
SATURDAY NIGHTS

IS SELDOM AT A
LOSS FOR WORDS

The Ten Least Popular Patron Saints

10. Saint Gulliver, patron saint of lawyers.

9. Saint Louella, patron saint of when Jesus' face appears somewhere strange and people go worship it.

8. Saint Genevieve, patron saint of insurance salesmen and ticks.

7. Saint Mortimer, patron saint of queasiness.

6. Saint Doris of Avila, patron saint of broken photocopiers.

5. Saint Malachi, patron saint of paper cuts.

4. Saint Garth of Rome, patron saint of humidity.

3. Saint Montgomery, patron saint of mislabelled food products.

2. Saint Otis, patron saint of polyester.

1. Saint Winifred, patron saint of liposuction.

Jonah's Top Ten Ways to Kill Time While Inside a Large Sea Creature

10. Sift through muck in search of valuables.

9. Plug your nose.

8. Sing showtunes.

7. Wish you'd brought a box of pepper or a dancing cricket.

6. Consider: "What would Abraham do?"

5. Think very seriously about whether tickling its esophagus would be a good idea.

4. Stay out of the stomach acids.

3. Count vertebrae.

2. Sing "Ninety-nine Bottles of Beer on the Stomach Wall."

1. Try to guess if it's a whale or just a big fish.

Top Ten Features of California Churches

10. Pews covered in genuine yak skin.

9. Indoor football field/Easter lawn.

8. Perrier fountain baptismal.

7. Communion wine is a 1968 Chablis.

6. Frequent missionary trips to Honolulu.

5. Instead of a church van, everyone gets their own church car.

4. Lobby contains world's largest Precious Children figurine.

3. Visitors get platinum-plated smiley-face pins.

2. Olympic-size, bean-sprout-shaped swimming pool.

1. Nursery gets cable.

Goliath's Top Ten Pet Peeves

10. People who say, "How's the weather up there?"

9. People who automatically expect you to be a good basketball player.

8. When your manager hires cheesy taunt writers.

7. Broccoli.

6. Chariots with low ceilings.

5. No one has quadruple-E sandals.

4. Always have to play Humbaba in annual Gilgamesh pageant.

3. Suspicion that there may be something dangerously wrong with your pituitary gland.

2. No matter what you wear, you still have that tall look.

1. Kids with slingshots.

Top Ten Courses at Christian Colleges

10. "What You Should Believe If You Ever Want to Graduate"

9. "Intermediate Spouse Hunting"

8. "Broadcasting"

7. "Advanced Legalism"

6. "Square Dancing" (cancelled)

5. "Seminar: Why Jesus Would Be Clean-Shaven Today"

4. "How to Tye a Tie"

3. "Brylcreem 101"

2. "Seminar: The History of Great Men God Has Threatened to Kill"

1. "Introduction to Non-Christians: What They Might Look Like"

Top Ten Titles for Christian Soap Operas

10. *All My Disciples*
 9. *A Better World*
 8. *Sharing*
 7. *The Young and the Celibate*
 6. *Search for Salvation*
 5. *As the World Counts Down to Armageddon*
 4. *One Faith to Follow*
 3. *St. Mary's Hospital*
 2. *This Present Darkness*
 1. *This Little Guiding Light of Mine*

LITTLE KNOWN MOMENTS
IN BIBLE HISTORY

#25

BUT, MOSES! BE REASONABLE! THINK OF YOUR LARGE PAGAN CONSTITUENCY!

Top Nine Exorcist Fears

9. Getting the giggles at a bad time.

8. Getting claw marks in brand-new furniture.

7. The demon will get sympathy by having a name like *Cuddles*.

6. The restraints will break and you'll have to use the cricket bat.

5. Being away when "60 Minutes" calls.

4. Getting heavy-breathing crank phone calls from unimaginative Satanists.

3. The pentagram on your business card will turn out smudged.

2. Neighbors complaining to police about screams and poltergeist activity.

1. One of your clients might get re-possessed.

TOP THREE QUALIFICATIONS FOR THE MODERN ELDER

A GOOD SUIT

BE ABLE TO STAND VERY STILL ALL THROUGH OFFERING <u>AND</u> COMMUNION

KNOW HOW TO ADJUST THE THERMOSTAT

Top Five Most Common Rhymes in Christian Songs

5. Love—above
4. Soul—whole
3. Life—strife
2. Sing—King
1. Lord—Word

Five Alternative Rhymes for Christian Songs

5. Love—shove or glove

4. Lord—snored or abhorred

3. Soul—Creole or bagarolle

2. Life—fife or rife

1. sing—anything (anything at all)

Top Ten Rejected Slogans of Christian Strong-Man Teams

10. "Convert or Be Pummeled"

9. "Spirit-filled, Steroid-Free"

8. "Can Mother Teresa Pop a Hot Water Bottle?"

7. "They Talk!"

6. "Come and Be Intimidated"

5. "Don't Miss the New Ice-Smashing Ministry!"

4. "Smell the Perspiration!"

3. "Like Christians, Only Stronger"

2. "Catch Grunt Fever!"

1. "Yes! We Have Grown Men in Tights Whacking Their Heads Against Bricks!"

PASTOR'S NIGHTMARE #13

PASTOR'S OFFICE

SECRETARY

OH, YEAH... SOME LADY NAMED DIANE SAWYER AND A GUY WITH A CAMERA HAVE BEEN IN THERE ALL MORNING WAITING FOR YOU...

Top Ten Things That Went Through Saint Francis' Mind When He Was on His Deathbed

10. "I hope I remembered to sign that 'Footprints' poem of mine."

9. "We're about the same size; they'll probably give my outfit to Brother Stu."

8. "This would be a bad time for my stigmata to reappear."

7. "I'd better call my wife in. Oops. I'm not married."

6. "I wish those birds would shut up."

5. "Dying in bed is boring, boring, boring."

4. "I wonder if I have time for one more game of badminton."

3. "Looking back on it all, I wish I hadn't gotten my head tonsured."

2. "I knew I shouldn't have eaten that taco."

1. "Is this an out-of-body experience, or am I just really, really dizzy?"

Top Nine Bible-Publisher Rejects

9. The "And Then There's Some Bad News" Bible.

8. The Reader's Digest Condensed New Testament (with Psalm and Proverb).

7. Scripture Lite (all "thou shalts" have been changed to "thou should try tos").

6. The Holy Writ Pop-Up Book.

5. The Rapper's Bible ("In the beginning: Word!").

4. The First-Year Greek Student Translation.

3. The California Version ("in the, like, beginning, you know . . .").

2. The Pig Latin Vulgate.

1. The Invisible Ink Bible with Secret Decoder Ring.

NAUGHTY CHILDREN'S TOP THREE TIPS FOR SABOTAGING A HOME GROUP MEETING

SPRINKLE DUST ON YOUR PARENT'S BIBLES

TUNE THE CLOCK RADIO IN TO A HEAVY METAL STATION AND SET IT TO COME ON FULL VOLUME DURING PRAYER

beer
cigarettes
red meat
Ghost Buster cereal
wine coolers

STICK A FAKE SHOPPING LIST ON THE FRIDGE

Top Ten Brand Names for Christian Perfumes

10. Original Sin
9. Transfiguration
8. Eau de Catacombs
7. The Wise Virgin
6. Sweet Hour of Prayer
5. Chastity
4. Gardens of Pomegranate
3. The Bondage of the Will
2. Jezebel!
1. Niceness

Top Ten Things Evangelical Protestants Can Learn from Catholics

10. Decorative use of candles.

9. Latin.

8. Art & architecture.

7. How to hold a church bazaar.

6. Celibacy.

5. Attracting ethnic minorities.

4. Reverence.

3. Exorcism.

2. Seeing Jesus' face in everyday objects.

1. Looking good in plaid uniforms.

Top Ten Things Catholics Can Learn from Evangelical Protestants

10. How to preach memorable sermons.

9. How to run a television station.

8. Hayrides.

7. Evangelism.

6. Recreational use of grape juice.

5. "Do-it-Yourself" doctrine.

4. "Amazing Grace" and "A Mighty Fortress."

3. Marketing Christian bumper stickers, Christian coin purses, Christian watches, Christian pens and so on.

2. How to tie a tie.

1. Using the Bible.

Friar Tuck's Top Ten Pet Peeves

10. Not being permitted to wear green tights.

9. Some days you just don't feel merry.

8. Tall people who poke your bald spot.

7. The merry men who never use their tithing envelopes.

6. Never getting the girl.

5. Trying to find a good place to sleep in the forest when it's raining.

4. Having all of your disguises as peasants blown because you're the only one wearing a large silver crucifix.

3. Frustration with the merry men slowly turning to Arianism.

2. Cheap Japanese cudgels.

1. Nagging feeling that "Thou shalt not steal."

Complete List of Social Issues Evangelicals Are Concerned About

2. Abortion

1. The destruction of the family

Top Ten Christian Game Shows

10. Name That Chorus

9. Wheel of Predestination

8. You Bet Your Soul

7. The Agape Connection

6. Squares

5. The Prophet Is Right

4. Christian Jeopardy

3. What's My Heresy?

2. The Newly Converted Game

1. Baptist Feud

TOP THREE
FUND RAISING FLOPS

SANCTUARY VENDORS

A HAIR WASH

A "HOLD-YOUR-BREATH-A-THON"

Nine Mormon Doctrines You Probably Didn't Know

9. It's okay to collect Coke memorabilia as long as it's blessed by an elder.

8. (tie) Donnie and Marie Osmond will become gods and make their music *forever*.
All Mormons have to like their music, but the especially devout are exempt from watching reruns of *Cocoanuts!*

7. Black people are really sophisticated holograms.

6. Heaven has wide, clean, well-maintained bike paths.

5. (Men only) You get extra credit in heaven each time you marry twin sisters.

4. God is about 5′ 9″, 165 pounds.

3. If non-Mormons ever actually saw a Temple wedding, they'd go blind or insane.

2. Not-so-good Mormons who become gods wind up ruling planets like Pluto.

1. At the end of time, Joseph Smith will stand before all the gathered faithful and say, "Just kidding!"

The Ten Least Popular Tracts from Raving Open-Air Press

10. *The UFOs That Are Reading My Brain*

9. *Evolution Is Stupid.*

8. *Proof That the Pope Is a Cannibal*

7. *Hell: What It Will Be Like*

6. *Rock Music and Vampirism: The Inevitable Connection*

5. *101 Reasons You Should Feel Bad for All You've Done*

4. *Burn, Papist, Burn!*

3. *Forgiveness?*

2. *Nasty Things That Will Happen If You Don't Convert Now*

1. *Are You the Antichrist?*

PASTOR'S NIGHTMARE
#42

REV. BOB HAD PASSED THE SEARCH COMMITTEE, THE BOARD OF ELDERS AND THE TRIAL SERMON... NOW IF HE COULD JUST MAKE IT THROUGH THE SWIM SUIT COMPETITION

Top Six Bible-Based Games That Never Quite Made It

7. Southern Baptist Chess (The liberal wing has to play red.)

6. Potluck Roulette

5. Bible Scrabble (Only words appearing in *Strong's Exhaustive Concordance* are used, and special rules permit Greek words and the Apocrypha.)

4. Christian Old Maid (In their twenties, the people on the cards pair off and raise Christian families. The loser becomes Minister to Singles.)

3. Televangelist Monopoly

2. Revelation Risk: Israel Versus Gog

1. Bible Dungeons & Dragons

Top Ten Ways to Detect Non-Christians

10. They're the ones who are always sinning.

9. 666 tattoo on their inner thighs.

8. They don't show up in mirrors.

7. They do good things for all the wrong reasons.

6. They wear black hats.

5. They hide a deep inner sadness.

4. They don't know the secret Christian handshake.

3. They swear sometimes.

2. When you toss them in water, they float.

1. If you ask them if they're Christians, they say no.

Top Ten Christian Slang Terms for the Rapture

10. Doing the Enoch
 9. The Ultimate Bungi Jump
 8. Helium Fallout
 7. The Last Laugh
 6. No More Catechism!
 5. Cloud Swimming
 4. Global Popcorn
 3. Finally Getting High
 2. Gravity Freakout
 1. The Rapturooni

ALTERNATIVE HOLIDAY TRADITION #6

INSTEAD OF HUNTING EGGS THIS EASTER... LIE STILL FOR THREE DAYS!

Top Eight Things Overheard at the Vatican

8. "He's a lot shorter without the hat."

7. "Don't be silly. Even if there *were* vampires, they wouldn't come *here*."

6. "The neighbors are complaining; you monks have to remember to chant *softly*."

5. "We're running low on fish."

4. "Bad news. There'll be 100,000 people showing up for the Pope's Easter message, and you and I have to hide the eggs."

3. "And now *this* chair's broken. Don't we have *anything* built after the 18th century?"

2. "Frankly, I'm tired of spaghetti."

1. "I don't care if you're a Franciscan. The rule is: No Pets!"

The Ten Most Common Questions Asked of Solomon

10. If Moses and Abraham got in a fistfight, who would win?

9. What do you mean my temples are like pomegranates?

8. Wanna play chess?

7. If an irresistible force meets an immovable object, does that really mean six more weeks of winter?

6. Can I have your autograph?

5. Can I have the Queen of Sheba's address?

4. What was your dad *really* like?

3. How do you maintain such a smooth complexion in all this heat?

2. When you first wrote your song, were you expecting it to go into the canon of Scripture?

1. If you're so smart, why don't you invent indoor plumbing for us?

LITTLE KNOWN MOMENTS
IN BIBLE HISTORY
17

WHAT REALLY HAPPENED TO LOT'S WIFE

The Six Least Popular Christian Family Videos

6. "We Never Talk Anymore: Families Who Just Watch Videotapes"

5. "Family Councils: An Introduction to Parliamentary Procedure"

4. "The Sound of Music"

3. " 'What Is My Child Saying?': A 'Hip' and 'Groovy' Guide to Teen 'Slang' "

2. "Raising Bail Quickly"

1. "When Your Child Is a Jerk"

Top Nine Sources of Friction in Adam and Eve's Marriage

9. Deciding what to call the platypus.

8. Adam's frequent comments like "All you women are the same."

7. Adam was a hunter; Eve was a gatherer.

6. Eve wanted to be called a "womyn."

5. Bickering over who had to get up and pick fig leaves.

4. Deciding whether or not to teach Cain and Abel at home using phonics.

3. (tie) Deciding who had to clean the first diaper.

Deciding who got to name whatever was *in* the first diaper.

2. Adam kept insisting that the whole Lilith thing was fictional. Eve would respond, "Then where did the story come from?"

1. Getting kicked out of Eden had to be *someone's* fault.

Top Seven Ways to Get Thrown Out of a Christian Theme Park

7. During break for refreshment, say loudly, "What's Christian about *this*? This is just ordinary, secular ice cream!"

6. Dangle your arms outside the car during the Dispensational Dioramas ride.

5. Yell "Darn you to *heck*!" so the guards can hear.

4. Make fun of the Christian basketball-shaped coin purses in the gift shop.

3. Pour eels down the water slide.

2. Sell your *own* Jesus belt buckles on the sidewalk.

1. When leaving, say loudly, "This stinks; let's go to Disneyland!"

PASTOR'S NIGHTMARE #6
"THE FREUDIAN SLIP"

TURN IN YOUR WALLETS WITH ME, IF YOU WILL, TO EXODUS 35...

Eight Outtakes from Dante's *Inferno*

8. The circle of disturbing fashion trends.

7. The circle where people turn into lobsters, but don't seem to mind especially.

6. The circle where, for all eternity, everyone sells Amway to one another.

5. The circle where everybody talks about their problems.

4. The circle of severe gum disease.

3. The special pit reserved for lawyers.

2. The circle for people who can't take a joke.

1. The limbo of unrenewed sitcoms.

Top Ten Rationalizations Christians Give for Sitting Through an R-rated Movie

10. It's art.

9. I have to learn how unbelievers live.

8. It's okay. One of the characters is a priest.

7. No, really it *is* art.

6. It doesn't affect me as long as I cross my arms and look displeased.

5. I'm just trying to figure out what they're doing.

4. This might be important to the plot later.

3. My *goodness,* is this artistic. . . .

2. I have to count the sex scenes if I'm going to report it to Don Wildmon.

1. It's either sit through this or rent *Chariots of Fire* again.

Top Ten Books Rejected by Christian Publishers

10. *The New Age Liberal Communist Plot to Steal Our Children and How Burning Your Senator Can Help*

9. *Two Thousand Reasons that Jesus Will Definitely, for Sure, No Doubt About It, Honest-to-Goodness RETURN in the Year 2000* (Reason #14: "It's a nice round number.")

8. *Ministering to the Christian Psychopath*

7. *C. S. Lewis' Collected Laundry Lists and Random Doodles*

6. *How to Do What's to Do When the Doing Has Been Done*

5. *How Women Cause Sin and What Young Men Can Do for Protection*

4. *The Book of Christian Golf Swings*

3. *Rock Music and Christian Houseplants: The Definitive Study*

2. *White Supremacy: A Biblical Approach*

1. *Controlling Your Thought Life by Reducing Its Volume*